W9-DGW-376

Handmade Homes

Handmade Homes

The Natural Way to Build Houses

ARTHUR BOERICKE
and
BARRY SHAPIRO

DELACORTE PRESS / NEW YORK

Published by
Delacorte Press
1 Dag Hammarskjold Plaza
New York, N.Y. 10017

Manufactured in the United States of America

First printing

Designed by Giorgetta Bell McRee

LIBRARY OF CONGRESS CATALOGING IN PUBLICATION DATA

Boericke, Art. Handmade homes.

1.   House construction.   2.   Dwellings.
I.   Shapiro, Barry, joint author.   II.   Title.
TH4812.B64   728.3′7   80-22607

ISBN 0-440-03340-3

This book is dedicated to my uncle, Charles Caleb Boericke, who got me started on carpentry at age fourteen.

It is also dedicated to many, many professional carpenters and lifelong members of the building trades: men such as Wilfred Lang, Roger Somers, Ken Howard, Pat Wall, and Jack Sward—men who taught me what skills I have, and men with whom I have spent so many useful and rewarding hours both on and off the job.

And lastly this book is dedicated to the ebullient builder-artist Jean Varda, the "Uncle Yanko" who constantly challenged the world of innocents, incorrigible hippopotami, and fashionable good taste.

ACKNOWLEDGMENTS

I would like to acknowledge the work of the many competent readers who have contributed their thoughts and criticisms both to this book and to several other volumes as yet unpublished. They are Barbara Weitz, Dianne Hall, Gent Sturgeon, Pete and Marion Owens, Virginia Gray, Marcia Dickinson, George and Mary Hoffman, Fred Andrews, Jim McAllister, Marc Larby, and Phyliss Lahargoue. At Delacorte I would like to thank my editor, Nick Ellison; the designer, Giorgetta McRee; and the copyeditor and proofreader, Debra Matteucci. That they could not correct all my errors is self-evident, but their efforts have eliminated all but the most gross and willful blunders—errors which I prefer to think of as my personal style.

The same can be said for Mori at *The Goodfellow Review of Crafts* and for the work of Susan Sherry Shapiro for her choice of the order of photographs and for her invaluable assistance to the entire project. The poet Stephen Ajay has my special thanks, for he gave the manuscript its final reading.

And through it all there has been the steadfast cooperation of Stephen's friend and my photographer and co-author, Barry. It has been an interesting but an almost profitless assignment for him, but notwithstanding that, he has carried this project forward in an ever more scrupulous and careful manner.

During the next year or two I may be able to begin the construction of a new home again, but till that time I am best reached through my agent, Helen Shapiro, 404 San Anselmo Avenue, San Anselmo, California 94960.

Five workmen cut, put together, and installed the three principal windows of this cabin—approximately 15, 16, and 20 square feet—in less than a week. Three of these men, Kim Hick, Lou Galetti, and Richard Evans, designed the windows. (They were also responsible for the remodeled State Office Building entry in San Francisco, and are very experienced in all phases of stained-glass work; but with a little instruction, an owner-builder can construct this sort of colorful three-dimensional window as easily as he can assemble the more conventional types, they tell me.)

OWNER: Deva Rajan
BUILDER: Deva Rajan
LOCATION: California, the San Francisco Bay area
OTHER CRAFTSMEN ON JOB: Carpenters—Ichikawasan, Gotosan, Barry Smith, Dean Pratt, Jeff Pratt, Seth Melchert, Michael Malott. Stained glass—Joan Machiz and Michael Lien. Built-in furniture and doors—Bruce Johnson.

DATE CONSTRUCTION BEGUN: 1964
DATE OF COMPLETION: in progress
YEARS LIVED IN: 5
COST OF CONSTRUCTION: $100,000
APPROXIMATE SQUARE FEET: 5,500 sq. ft. of living area
                        2,000 sq. ft. of deck

MAXIMUM WINTER TEMPERATURE: 70°
AVERAGE WINTER TEMPERATURE: 50°
MAXIMUM SUMMER TEMPERATURE: 100°
AVERAGE SUMMER TEMPERATURE: 70°
AVERAGE WINTER HEATING BILL: $200
TYPE OF HEAT: wood stove and propane gas

Deva's three-story home underlines his careful use of light and shade, and his intuitive understanding of the male and female principles that permeate classic architecture.

One by one, the stained-glass windows were designed right on the job-site by two craftsmen, Joan Machiz and Michael Lien, who leased the home in Deva's absence and used the lower floor as their workshop and studio.

Deva Rajan is a licensed contractor. In 1973 his Canyon Construction Company faithfully restored Fort Ross, an early Russian settlement. Currently he spends several months each year working on a Hindu temple; and like myself, he has also been an instructor at the California College of Arts and Crafts.

OWNERS: Scott and Nancy Lamb
BUILDERS: Scott and Nancy Lamb
LOCATION: Taney County, Missouri*
OTHER CRAFTSMEN ON JOB: none

DATE CONSTRUCTION BEGUN: 1973
DATE OF COMPLETION: 1975
YEARS LIVED IN: 5
COST OF CONSTRUCTION: $6,000
APPROXIMATE SQUARE FEET: 950 sq ft., approx. 9,000 cu. ft.

LOWEST WINTER TEMPERATURE: —25°
AVERAGE WINTER TEMPERATURE: 25°
MAXIMUM SUMMER TEMPERATURE: 102°
AVERAGE SUMMER TEMPERATURE: 80°
MAXIMUM VELOCITY WIND AND SEASON: 20 mph
AVERAGE WINTER HEATING BILL: 0
MAXIMUM WINTER HEATING BILL: 0
TYPE OF HEAT: wood (fireplace)

MATERIALS: 6 x 6 pine timbers, rough-sawed pine ceilings, oak floors, lime-stone fireplace

COMMENTS: Every aspect of construction, rock, wood, stained glass, plumbing, and cabinetry was done by us. We had no previous experience before this house.

---

* Unlike their neighbors, the Lambs chose to locate down by the creek, where it is a good deal colder than on the bluffs and ridgetops. There, in a deciduous grove of trees that lets the sun in during the two coldest months and shades them during the much longer summer, they have built a home that is so well insulated that it stays warm and toasty when the air is 10 to 15 degrees colder than on the uplands, and where they can take advantage of this differential during the remainder of the year. If it heats up too much nonetheless, they can open a vent at the roof peak and exhaust the excess heat—very much like Jonathan Grumette does in North Carolina and Gary Noffke does down in Georgia.

As you approach this small home, it seems to be a simple log shanty, and nothing more. But when you walk inside, you quickly see that it is a fancy two-story octagon that "just happens" to fit in with the old-time farmhouses that are down the road.

OWNERS: Doris and Michael Taylor
BUILDERS: Tom Brady, with assistance of Karen Terry, Peter Dousan, and Mark Fricke
LOCATION: northern New Mexico
OTHER CRAFTSMEN ON JOB: John McKinney, Bruce Davis, Dennis Visil

DATE REMODELING BEGUN: 1977
DATE OF COMPLETION: Spring 1978
YEARS LIVED IN: 2
COST OF CONSTRUCTION: $44,000
APPROXIMATE SQUARE FEET: 1,100 sq. ft.

MAXIMUM WINTER TEMPERATURE: in sun-room (living room), mid 70's and other parts of house, mid 60's, without any backup system during day
AVERAGE WINTER TEMPERATURE: mid to upper 40's in sun-room and 50's in rest, without using wood stove
MAXIMUM SUMMER TEMPERATURE: upper 70's
AVERAGE SUMMER TEMPERATURE: upper 60's, low 70's
MAXIMUM VELOCITY WIND AND SEASON: 40–50 mph, spring
                                    25 mph, rest of year
AVERAGE WINTER HEATING BILL: $30–40 per month, including cost of wood (down to $20 when we cut our own)
MAXIMUM WINTER HEATING BILL: $45 per month
TYPE OF HEAT: passive solar adobe with wood-stove backup, hot-water electric baseboard in bathroom only

MATERIALS: flagstone, local rock, pine, brick floors

This old adobe makes excellent use of the odd nooks and loft spaces that were created by its periodic remodeling. The new sun-room and hot-water heater have transformed this ancient home into a modern town house whose simple lines belie its efficient use of energy.

A reflector increases the area that is exposed to the sun's heat and allows the watertank to be placed directly on the *vigas* over the kitchen —a location that not only places it near the sink and bath and laundry, but also provides the resident with an easy-to-maintain, direct-gain hotwater system.

The cabinets and doors are by John McKinney, one of the nation's most respected craftsmen and tutor to generations of young woodworkers. The general contractor, Tom Brady, has supervised many of the best-known Karen Terry jobs, and his ability to inspire thoughtful proper craftsmanship should serve as a model for every southwestern contractor.

OWNER: Jonathan Grumette
BUILDER: Jonathan Grumette
LOCATION: Chatham County, North Carolina
OTHER CRAFTSMEN ON JOB: Carpentry by Eddie and Mark Hauser, Andy Fleishman, Mark Gurley, Dave Smith, Jim Lakiotes, and Steve Erickson. Cabinetmaker: Bill Mason. Details by Susan Katherine Smith, Jim Janty, and Tim McDowell. Tiles by Jane Bomberg, plastering by Albert Regester. Susanna Stewart, stained-glass maker. Murals by Jim Frisino. Larry Green, mason.

DATE CONSTRUCTION BEGUN: February 1978
DATE OF COMPLETION: February 1980
YEARS LIVED IN: 1
COST OF CONSTRUCTION: $89,250
APPROXIMATE SQUARE FEET: 1,050 sq. ft.

MAXIMUM WINTER TEMPERATURE: 70's
AVERAGE WINTER TEMPERATURE: mid 40's–50's
MAXIMUM SUMMER TEMPERATURE: 100°
AVERAGE SUMMER TEMPERATURE: mid 80's–90's
MAXIMUM VELOCITY WIND AND SEASON: 40 mph, March
AVERAGE WINTER HEATING BILL: not yet known
MAXIMUM WINTER HEATING BILL: not yet known
TYPE OF HEAT: wood stove, gas furnace backup

MATERIALS: frame, interior walls of aged wood and plaster

COMMENTS: "I wanted to build a great house—something so pure, it was human. I have breathed my life into it. Sometimes, late at night, I would say prayers aloud to imbue the walls with those special words in remembrance of God. What an adventure it has been—how very fortunate I am."

Nothing has been borrowed here. That is, there hasn't been a conscious or deliberate borrowing; yet the humid Carolina summers have suggested, I think, the sliding doors, and they have in turn created a somewhat Japanese-looking facade. While the clean, precise detailing, the immaculate craftsmanship, and the general airiness may certainly remind one of Japan's best domestic architecture, you should notice, if you will, the vents built into the brick chimneyside—an experiment by the young designer-builder that has no precedent that I know of in the Orient.

OWNERS: Herb and Marcy Balderson
BUILDER: Herb Balderson
LOCATION: Pitkin County, Colorado
OTHER CRAFTSMEN ON JOB: Bobby Balderson

DATE CONSTRUCTION BEGUN: 1973
DATE OF COMPLETION: 1975
YEARS LIVED IN: 7
COST OF CONSTRUCTION: $20,000
APPROXIMATE SQUARE FEET: 2,000 sq. ft.

MAXIMUM WINTER TEMPERATURE: 50°
AVERAGE WINTER TEMPERATURE: 25°
MAXIMUM SUMMER TEMPERATURE: 90°
AVERAGE SUMMER TEMPERATURE: 65°
MAXIMUM VELOCITY WIND: 30 mph (rarely)
AVERAGE WINTER HEATING BILL: $500
MAXIMUM WINTER HEATING BILL: $600
TYPE OF HEAT: natural gas—wood

MATERIALS: slip form with brick, railroad ties as beams, 3 x 6 decking, glass

It takes a good deal of firewood to offset the glass in the upstairs living room and the room below, but the builder wanted to be constantly aware of this beautiful alpine meadow, and to enjoy the evening view of the town, and also the mountains, where he often skiis.

OWNERS: Nicholas Morrow and Adrienne Arias Morrow
BUILDERS: Nicholas Morrow and Adrienne Arias Morrow, Andrea Romero de Arias, Chuck Banner, David Rossiter, Ann Feldmeir, Chuck Rossiter, Ramon Lopez, Bob and Alice and *many* sweet friends
LOCATION: northern New Mexico
OTHER CRAFTSMEN ON JOB: The Browns, Michael Walker, Pepe, Pierre, Baird Banner

DATE CONSTRUCTION BEGUN: 1971
DATE OF COMPLETION: Will it ever?
YEARS LIVED IN: 7
COST OF CONSTRUCTION: $30,000
APPROXIMATE SQUARE FEET: growhole, 1,500 sq. ft.
home, 2,200 sq. ft.

MAXIMUM WINTER TEMPERATURE: 35°–40°
AVERAGE WINTER TEMPERATURE: 15°
MAXIMUM SUMMER TEMPERATURE: 90°–95°
AVERAGE SUMMER TEMPERATURE: 85°
MAXIMUM VELOCITY WIND: 35–45 (approx.)
AVERAGE WINTER HEATING BILL: 4–5 cords wood (piñon), gas for truck, fuel for chainsaw, and great fall air
TYPE OF HEAT: wood—cookstove in kitchen, three fireplaces, and heating stove

MATERIALS:
mud, from the excavated hole where we built our house.
straw, some from our field, some from others.
vigas, large cedar and aspen beams from the mountains that oversee and protect our lands, whose changing leaf colors tell us what "time" it is from afar.
latillas, smaller aspen poles.
stone, some from the upper valley (thanks to Uncle Larry), a bit of lava from the gorge. But most of the smooth and round river rock is from the gully just below the house site.
brick, large to tiny, each one special and unique, finding its way to fireplace, window bed and delicately detailed niche. Looking for stone on a bright day was like hunting for Easter eggs! The magic one experienced on that land and its colors was nothing less.
clay, dug from special places across the way for the final *alisandro*, the slip finish on adobe walls that brings a color so delicate only the earth mother creates it. The work, traditionally done by women, was for us a time of centering, with wall and clay and each other.
tamarisk boughs, deep red and willowy. They, instead of *latillas*, form the hall entrance ceiling.
glass, Plexiglas glazing, corrugated plastic (growhole roof).
milled woods, on shelving and counter spaces only.

COMMENTS: Four fifths of the materials for the growhole house were gathered from the immediate or neighboring area. Building it was a community experience. For a period of time, in the beginning, students from the Taos Learning Center (high school age) provided much help, and in this way they fulfilled the requirements for their apprenticeship program at the school. Later on friends came over to lend a hand.

Our community is made up of five craftsmen and artists, people strongly committed to the land. Natural resources play a major part in the life-style here. Water and wood are precious. The growhole helps us to constantly attune ourselves to the seasons that govern and give—to attune ourselves and be grateful.

Another pioneering greenhouse-home called, appropriately enough, "The Growhole." The rockwork is so exceptional here that the builder, a professional potter and jeweler, was offered employment as a full-time mason only a few months after he began this home.

The roof is being rebuilt this autumn. Though economic in both its concept and execution, it did not properly insulate the home, and it cut off the mountains to the south. In the words of Adrienne: "Now we'll see Truchas Peak through the growhole proper. The winters will be a lot warmer in the house, and the summers cooler too [for ventilation was a problem in the past]." Prospective builders should take heed: even a well-built, well-thought-out design will have its share of problems.

OWNER: Gary L. Noffke
BUILDER: Gary L. Noffke; James A. Mitchell, De Land, Florida, architect
LOCATION: North Georgia
OTHER CRAFTSMEN ON JOB: Stained-glass window—glass made by Fritz Dreisbach; window designed and constructed by Fritz Dreisbach, Rene Guerin, Gary Noffke, Mary Manusos

DATE CONSTRUCTION BEGUN: 1973
DATE OF COMPLETION: 1974
YEARS LIVED IN: 6
COST OF CONSTRUCTION: $45,000
APPROXIMATE SQUARE FEET: 1,500 sq. ft.

LOWEST WINTER TEMPERATURE: 5°
AVERAGE WINTER TEMPERATURE: 40°
MAXIMUM SUMMER TEMPERATURE: 95° day, 70° night
AVERAGE SUMMER TEMPERATURE: 78°
MAXIMUM VELOCITY WIND: 10
AVERAGE WINTER HEATING BILL: $50
MAXIMUM WINTER HEATING BILL: $75
TYPE OF HEAT: wood primary, electric secondary, gas (optional)

MATERIALS: cedar 3 x 6 T&G

This very successful Georgia A-frame is an architect-designed variation of great foresight and common sense. By opening the home lengthwise to the broad deck and the swiftly flowing stream, he has solved two vexing problems: This A-frame is far better ventilated that those that are open only at the gables or along their ridge, and the major living areas have better access and circulation.

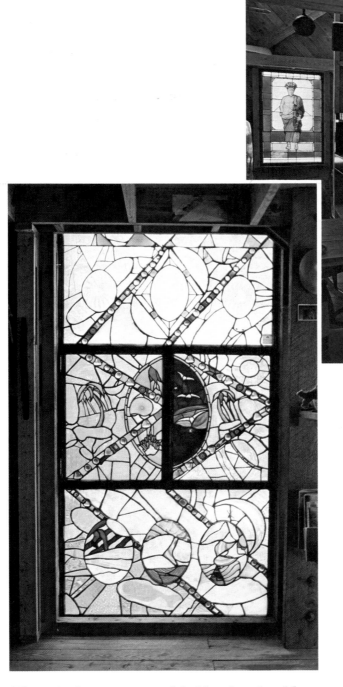

This window was assembled by the glassblower and three fellow crafts-men. Its panels are already well-known in the trade for they demon-strate how individual pieces of handsome hand-blown glass can be worked into an elaborate, well-organized whole without distorting the overall design.

OWNERS: Marie Ouhrabka/Don Henley
BUILDERS: Don Young/Jon Wild and company involved in finishing work
LOCATION: Aspen, Colorado
OTHER CRAFTSMEN ON JOB: many, many friends

DATE RECONSTRUCTION BEGUN: 1972
DATE OF COMPLETION: 1978
YEARS LIVED IN: 7
APPROXIMATE SQUARE FEET: 2,800 sq. ft.

WINTER TEMPERATURE: —20° to 40°
SUMMER TEMPERATURE: 30° to 92°
AVERAGE WINTER HEATING BILL: too much
TYPE OF HEAT: wood and electric baseboard

MATERIALS: river and lichen rock, ferrocement, brick, iron, and recycled wood

COMMENTS: When we discovered this place in 1972, it was an old broken-down homestead that was without windows, doors, chinking, and parts of the roof.

The basic construction would have been impossible without the help of my many friends, though Don Young and Jon Wild were the principal craftsmen for the finished work. David Hauter was the architect who interpreted my designs.

Imaginative bold designs and rugged contrasting materials are woven into a unified, coherent pattern in this completely remodeled Colorado homestead. Note, moreover, that the new ferrocement stairway would be either too costly or too cumbersome-looking in plain concrete; and that despite the owner's crediting the work to her many friends, the patterns created by the brick and ironwork are hardly casual after-thoughts or happy Sunday accidents.

OWNER: Gale Walker
BUILDER: Howard Orem
LOCATION: Humbolt County, California
OTHER CRAFTSMEN ON JOB: none

DATE CONSTRUCTION BEGUN: 1974
DATE OF COMPLETION: 1975
YEARS LIVED IN: 4
COST OF CONSTRUCTION: $20,000
APPROXIMATE SQUARE FEET: 1,800 sq. ft.

WINTER TEMPERATURE: O.S. 32°–I.S. 55°
AVERAGE WINTER TEMPERATURE: O.S. 50°–I.S. 70°
SUMMER TEMPERATURE: O.S. 80°–I.S. 70°
AVERAGE SUMMER TEMPERATURE: O.S. 60°–I.S. 70°
MAXIMUM WIND VELOCITY: 60 mph
AVERAGE WINTER HEATING BILL: 0
MAXIMUM WINTER HEATING BILL: 0
TYPE OF HEAT: solar and wood

MATERIALS: natural wood and stone, 90% coming from the property

Howard Orem's very straightforward Spartan greenhouse-home is located in a mild fogbound coastal area—hence the good-sized wood heater that serves as a backup to the solar-heating system. Always modest and unassuming, Howard has very little to say about this new greenhouse yet, but he does cover the purchase and maintenance of rural property, and some of the more practical aspects of organic farming in his book *Country Land* (Naturegraph Publishers, Inc., Box 1075, Happy Camp, Calif. 96039, or available directly from Soluna, Box 50, Petrolia, Calif. 95558; $9.00 hardcover, $5.00 paperback).

OWNERS: Jock and Maggie Lauterer
BUILDERS: Jock and Maggie Lauterer
LOCATION: Hogwild, Rutherford County, North Carolina
OTHER CRAFTSMEN ON JOB: Mike Thompson, Carlton Mason, Charlie Radcliff, Bill and Jeanette Byers—all carpenter friends who assisted or advised. Claude and Elaine Graves made kitchen tiles. Cabinets by Mountaineer Crafts of Cove Creek.

DATE CONSTRUCTION BEGUN: 1974
DATE OF COMPLETION: June 1978
YEARS LIVED IN: 3
COST OF CONSTRUCTION: $10,000. This is difficult to say, since the bulk of the materials was salvaged. Our windows were the most expensive item, since all are good Thermopane ones, mostly crank-outs.
APPROXIMATE SQUARE FEET: 1,200 sq. ft. Center room is 18′ x 22′ with an 18 ft. ceiling.

LOWEST WINTER TEMPERATURE: 8°
AVERAGE WINTER TEMPERATURE: 35°
MAXIMUM SUMMER TEMPERATURE: 95°
AVERAGE SUMMER TEMPERATURE: 80°
AVERAGE VELOCITY WIND AND SEASON: We built in a valley so this would not be a factor. The only wind we're exposed to is from the south.
AVERAGE WINTER HEATING BILL: $0, except when we turn on auxiliary electric heat in children's rooms, but this is only when it's very cold.
TYPE OF HEAT: wood heat and passive solar with large Thermopane windows on southeast and south sides that heat house from 9 A.M. to 5 P.M. in winter. Insulation in a home makes *all* the difference in retaining these heat sources.

MATERIALS: heart pine cut prior to 1850 (logs, floor, wall paneling) and Surewall, a plaster-Fiberglas combination. Cedar shakes from the stone roof and upper outside walls. Chestnut for railings, and salvage pine for board and batten.

COMMENTS: You gotta have heart—and in our case, heart pine. The 150-year-old log barn was labeled and disassembled and moved log by log 500 feet to the new site, where more heart pine (from a nearby tenant house I'd spent one summer salvaging) fleshed out floors and walls.

Rockwork—chimney, hearth, and wood stove's rock cubbyhole—all the result of bodacious beginner's enthusiasm. I do believe if the newspaper ever becomes obsolete that's what I'd do—rocking on.

The main thing about the whole Hogwild experience is our growing affection for building—rebuilding, molding *old* buildings, borrowing from the tradition they embody and suggest while adding freely the features available to us today—plaster,

Situated on the edge of the hot, humid southeastern plain, in December this foothill site is cold enough to warrant the seeming extravagance of Thermopane—the builder's principal expense, indeed.

---

insulated "chinking." There is a feeling of the continuity of time—roots, if you will. The feeling one gets by building and then living deep in this heart-pine embrace.

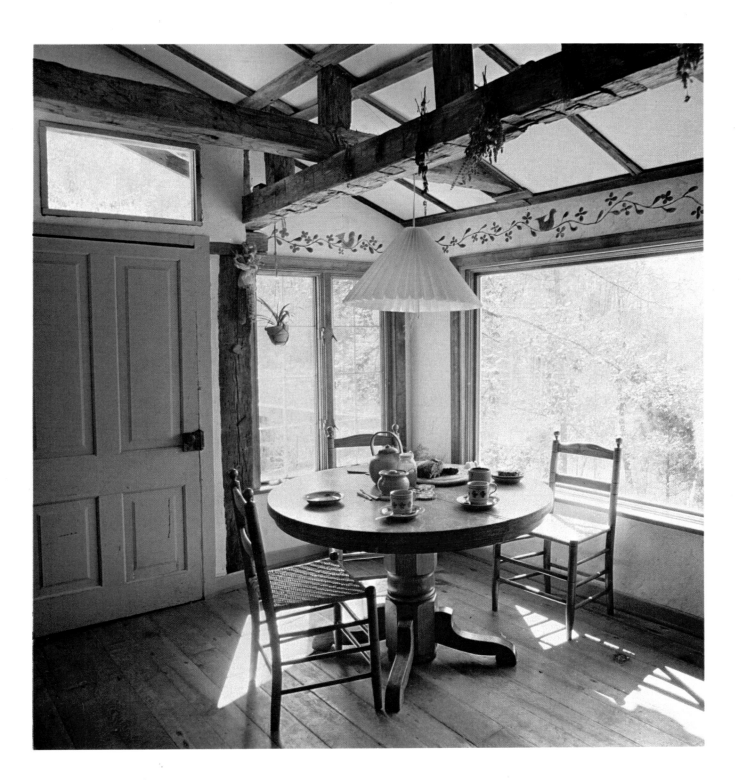

If you construct your home with a little respect for both its neighbors and its site, a solar design need not look like an army barracks or a housing project. When using recycled salvaged logs, for instance, you can rearrange them on the south and thus admit more winter sun and summer light.

OWNERS: Barbara and Frank Finn
BUILDERS: Gary Brodmerkel and Paul Melamud
LOCATION: Gold Hill, Boulder, Colorado
OTHER CRAFTSMEN ON JOB: none

DATE CONSTRUCTION BEGUN: 1973
DATE OF COMPLETION: 1974
YEARS LIVED IN: ½
COST OF CONSTRUCTION: $18,000, to remodel cabin and build greenhouse and kitchen
APPROXIMATE SQUARE FEET: n/a

ELEVATION: 8,300 ft.
WINTER TEMPERATURE: —30°–50°
SUMMER TEMPERATURE: 50°–90°
MAXIMUM VELOCITY WIND AND SEASON: 100 mph, winter
TYPE OF HEAT: wood, solar, and two small electric baseboard heaters in greenhouse

This pioneering greenhouse-home has a pond for aquaculture as well as the more usual gardenside amenities and rebuilt kitchen. Having stood the test of time in one of the northern hemisphere's most severe winter climates, it is an excellent prototype for those who wish to construct a like-minded structure.

OWNER: Jon Wild
BUILDER: Jon Wild
LOCATION: Aspen, Colorado
OTHER CRAFTSMEN ON JOB: none

DATE CONSTRUCTION BEGUN: June 1970
DATE OF COMPLETION: June 1982
YEARS LIVED IN: 3
COST OF CONSTRUCTION: $20,000
APPROXIMATE SQUARE FEET: 1,000 sq. ft.

LOWEST WINTER TEMPERATURE: −15°
AVERAGE WINTER TEMPERATURE: 20°
MAXIMUM SUMMER TEMPERATURE: 90°
AVERAGE SUMMER TEMPERATURE: 75°
MAX. VELOCITY WIND AND SEASON: 20 mph, spring
AVERAGE WINTER HEATING BILL: $20
MAXIMUM WINTER HEATING BILL: $30
TYPE OF HEAT: natural-gas-fired boiler, hot water radiated slab floors

MATERIALS: The exterior skin is a ¾″ ferrocement shell with an overlay of 2 inches of styro and sod. The interior ⅛″ plaster shell covers 2 inches of sprayed cellulose and 1 inch of styro beads. With this insulation in place, the home has turned out to be snug and comfortable through the Colorado winters.

Ten years of experimenting is the basis for this unique and inge-
niously designed small home—but note that an adequately insulated,
properly thought-out ferrocement structure is not necessarily the quick-
est or the least expensive way to build.

OWNER: Redwoods Abbey, cloister
BUILDER: Bob McKee; and Michael Crowe, architect
LOCATION: Mendocino County, California
OTHER CRAFTSMEN ON JOB: Richard Gienger and Joseph Gerspacher

DATE CONSTRUCTION BEGUN: 1972
DATE OF COMPLETION: Spring 1973
YEARS LIVED IN: 6½
COST OF CONSTRUCTION: $6,000
APPROXIMATE SQUARE FEET: n/a

WINTER TEMPERATURE: 18°–65°
AVERAGE WINTER TEMPERATURE: 50°
SUMMER TEMPERATURE: 35°–115°
AVERAGE SUMMER TEMPERATURE: 70°
MAXIMUM VELOCITY WIND AND SEASON: 30–40 mph, winter storms; 2–3 mph, summer afternoons
AVERAGE WINTER HEATING BILL: $150
MAXIMUM WINTER HEATING BILL: $200
TYPE OF HEAT: electric baseboard/*Jøtvl* stove

MATERIALS: old growth redwood

This small cabin is in the cloister of a monastic community and is a remarkable example of a builder's ability not only to follow the letter of his contractual obligations, but also to amplify and beautifully fulfill the architect's real intent.

OWNER: Lama Foundation
BUILDERS: Overall design: Steve Durkee and friends
Main dome and kitchen dome: Zomes (framing) by Steve Baer
LOCATION: Taos County, New Mexico
OTHER CRAFTSMEN ON JOB: not known

DATE CONSTRUCTION BEGUN: 1967
DATE OF COMPLETION: 1971
YEARS LIVED IN: 11
APPROXIMATE SQUARE FEET: main dome 46′ diameter octagon with wings

LOWEST WINTER TEMPERATURE: −30°
AVERAGE WINTER TEMPERATURE: 40°
MAXIMUM SUMMER TEMPERATURE: 95°
AVERAGE SUMMER TEMPERATURE: 60°
MAXIMUM VELOCITY WIND AND SEASON: 50–60 mph, March
AVERAGE WINTER HEATING BILL: separate figures not available for individual buildings
TYPE OF HEAT: wood

Lama is a private retreat and study center. At 9,000 feet the building season is very short and the foundation's inspired building program has required year upon year of persevering labor and the very frugal use of a limited endowment.